ADOPTION

The Essential Guide

Diana Cambridge

Adoption - The Essential Guide is also available in accessible formats for people with any degree of visual impairment. The large print edition and eBook (with accessibility features enabled) are available from Need2Know. Please let us know if there are any special features you require and we will do our best to accommodate your needs.

First published in Great Britain in 2012 by
Need2Know
Remus House
Coltsfoot Drive
Peterborough
PE2 9BF
Telephone 01733 898103
Fax 01733 313524
www.need2knowbooks.co.uk

Contents

Introduction

I'll never forget the first day I saw Clare. I'd barely slept the night before. Years of waiting, despairing, hoping and false starts were (I hoped) to be finally rewarded.

She was eight, living with foster parents and ran down to meet us as our car bumped up the lane to her foster home in Devon. I knew instantly that this smiling, lovely little girl would be our daughter, even though we were still on the first awkward steps towards adoption.

I could hardly speak for emotion.

Fast-forward twenty years! We're like all other parents – proud of Clare's success (deputy manager of a flagship Top Shop in Bath) dealing with the regular appeals for financial bail outs, always on red alert to offer advice or help or give a lift.

We're used to the long absences between phone calls and visits, (even though we live in the same city) and the sudden pop-up texts 'Can u lend me £50 till pay day? Thanx! Cx'.

If you're thinking of adopting, there's never been a better time. Though the process will never be as fast as you'd like, the government has now forcefully endorsed adoption, shortened all the procedures and insisted that local authorities make it easier to adopt and speed up processes. Red tape is being reduced. A child can now be freed for adoption and placed with adoptive parents within one year. As a prospective adopter, you'll be welcomed.

We will never regret adopting Clare, despite some turbulent times! It's so nice to treat her now and then to a lunch in Café Rouge or Pizza Express, maybe talking about the past – that first meeting, her moving in, the honeymoon period followed by (seemingly endless) years of quarrels and sulks.

We can look back on the rows, the fallings out, the reconciliations. But now the steady love and friendship is maintained. We've come through adoption, the three of us.

So if you're planning to adopt, or in the process of adopting, this book takes you through all the practical and emotional stages you'll encounter. Step by step, I explain them simply and offer advice from my own experience and errors – and I made plenty of mistakes!

It's these which cause the most pain and, if I'd had a book like this at my side, perhaps the bad times wouldn't have made me so low. My handbook highlights the tricky stages and offers ideas on how to tackle them, as well as giving all the practical and informative detail.

The hardest part of the adoption process is certainly the start. It can be lonely. It's not easy to acknowledge and reveal that you plan to adopt. The average age of children placed with adoptive families is four years: there are few babies.

When you tell them your plan, family and friends aren't always as helpful as they could be. And often there's no end in sight.

But . . . it's still easier to adopt than ever before. Everything is on your side. What you do need is stamina to power you through the waiting, emotional resilience to get you through the approval process, energy to embark on the first year and realistic expectations – it won't be a bed of roses all the way!

What it will be is infinitely rewarding and marvellous to look back on. When you've adopted a child, you've done something totally worthwhile. You've been generous with your love, and that love will be returned.

Being a parent is also fun and enjoyable, maybe more so if your boy or girl is adopted. And your child is likely to flourish – statistics show adopted children often do so much better than children who remain in care.

I completely recommend adopting a child. This book will route you through the legal maze, and support you through the emotional upheavals. It explains complex issues with clarity.

Whether you are thinking about adopting, have begun the process, are working with adoptive families or coming to terms with that first year – this book can be your guide.

It's dedicated with love to everyone on that demanding but joyous journey.

Chapter One

First Steps

You've decided to investigate adopting a child. This decision should be exciting and thrilling. Probably it will be – but don't be surprised if, at first, it isn't! My memory of finally making the decision to go along to an introductory adoption group was that, as a childless woman, I felt reluctant to go. I wasn't looking forward to it.

Whatever the reason, driving to Durham on an icy cold spring evening wasn't easy . . . yet the minute I entered the room and saw other faces as nervous, yet smiling, as my own, everything changed. The social workers couldn't have been more welcoming. Other would-be adopters were friendly. After that first evening, everything fell into place. I felt uplifted and on the start of a fundamental journey.

Start right now!

It's a journey you can begin now. Look on the Internet or in the Yellow Pages to find agencies near you, or contact your local authority and the voluntary adoption agencies in your area. To locate one near you, log on to the website of the British Association for Adoption and Fostering (BAAF), which has a find an agency directory (see the help list). BAAF will welcome your interest. It will send you an information pack about adoption, and details of some of the children needing new families.

Our adopted girl

That first evening in chilly Durham changed my life. We were assessed and approved, and after a wait of two years, we adopted Clare, then aged eight. She, her younger brother and small sister were all in care and looking for families, ideally near to each other, and all of them were adopted by families living in the West Country (where we'd moved to from Durham). As a childless couple in our early forties, having Clare was tremendously exciting for us.

Clare was a delightful little girl, healthy and bright, but with some emotional difficulties stemming from a background of severe neglect. She was never expected to be outstanding – 'unwise to expect too much' her foster parents warned – but today she is deputy manager of a high street fashion store, in charge of training, recruitment, payroll for 70 staff – and only a step away from having her own store to manage.

I believe the foster parents were right to be cautious about her prospects. Having too-high expectations for any child is, I think, a big mistake parents often make. For an adopted child to be in good psychological and physical shape and most importantly happy and achieving their potential – that's plenty to ask for!

You'd be amazed just how successful adopted children can be, despite the damaging effects of their early life – if you are prepared to put up with some draining and exhausting times during adolescence.

Having survived the turbulence of the teenage years, I can say it was a wonderful thing to do, and a privilege. I couldn't have asked for a lovelier girl. You will find that there are many children in care who are talented in all sorts of ways, all children to be proud of.

'There has never been a better time to think about adoption. The government has said the process until now has been "painfully slow" it has promised to do all it can to improve it.'

Government go-ahead

There has never been a better time to think about adoption. The government has said the process until now has been 'painfully slow' it has promised to do all it can to improve it. It has pledged to speed up the adoption system, and wants to see many more children adopted.

Though checks will continue to be rigorous, they will not be overprescriptive, which means that rules on who can and can't adopt – in terms of age, race, health, habits (such as smoking) will be relaxed.

This is very encouraging if you want to adopt children in the four-plus age range. But adopting babies will still be relatively difficult. The number of babies freed for adoption is small. The average age of children adopted in Britain is four years.

Cared for children

The fact is that most of the children in care have not been placed there voluntarily – they have been removed from their birth families by social service departments because of neglect (including malnutrition) and abuse.

Don't be surprised if some of your friends, when you tell them of your plans, will imagine that you are adopting a baby given up reluctantly by a healthy young girl from a good family. They might sympathise with the mother, imagining that her baby has been taken from her against her will. That's how adoption was back in the 20th century. But now there is no stigma around being a single mother, hardly any newborns need to be adopted.

Babies given up by birth mothers and made available for adoption – extremely uncommon these days – are called 'relinquished babies'. Foundlings are abandoned children and babies who remain unclaimed.

Railway children

I worked with a girl who was abandoned thirty years ago, at the age of four, with her brother of three at Temple Meads railway station in Bristol. They sat on a bench with their bags until they were noticed by station staff. They were successfully adopted. These cases are rare, but still happen. Authorities make every effort to trace the mother, but don't always succeed.

'The average age of children adopted in Britain is four years.'

My husband, David Kernek, was adopted in 1947 just six months after his birth. His mother was an Austrian refugee living in London. The adoption was arranged privately; her GP knew of a childless couple desperate to adopt. With just a few cursory checks, and no attempt at matching, perhaps it was just luck that the couple, who lived in very modest flat, were loving and kind parents.

David managed to trace his birth mother, Greta, when he was in his 50s – and only did so after his adoptive mother had died. It took him two years of perseverance and more than 120 letters and contacts before he found his way to her house in North London. After her initial shock, she and David formed a close and loving bond up until her death fifteen years later.

Finding families

'Most of the children awaiting adoption in the UK have suffered some form of serious neglect or abuse within their birth family.'

There is some idea that social workers 'find' children for families who long for them. That's not what happens; it's entirely the other way round. Their job is to find everlasting parents for children who need them. And currently, only five percent of children in care – sometimes known as looked-after children – are adopted each year.

Most of the children awaiting adoption in the UK have suffered some form of serious neglect or abuse within their birth family. It could have been emotional, physical (including not being dressed or fed properly) or sexual.

As adopters, you will receive a full report of your child's history. It won't be light reading. You need to be able to cope with the weight of their sad life so far . . . but remember that as children, they are probably more resilient emotionally than you!

Safe house

So, your adopted child will most likely have a background of neglect. Social workers, when they are aware of the damaging family circumstances, do all they can to help the birth mother, sometimes by sending someone to go every day to the family, helping and teaching the mother to cook, clean and care for her children.

This was Clare's experience, and she has a memory of the helper showing her mother how to bake bread, with the children joining in.

But if the carer's efforts do not succeed and the problems continue, the children will eventually be removed from the birth home and taken to a place of safety. Older adopted children will have this strong memory – of being removed from their home by strangers.

If older children in the family have already been taken into care, the authorities may move faster – they will already be concerned about the mother's abilities to keep her other children safe and well.

Safety first

The primary reason for the removal of the children is to ensure their safety, and it is carried out in as kind and sensitive a manner as possible. Yet for the children it's bound to be traumatic.

Age no barrier

Adoption agencies are now in competition for adoptive parents and their guidelines are far less prescriptive than they used to be. There are no blanket bans.

The health and safety of the chid is the main interest – there must be no risk attached to the placement. If you smoke, it would be unlikely for a pre-schooler to be placed with you – it will not be in the child's best interests. But for an older child – and all else being equal – smoking should be no barrier.

'If you are interested in adoption and willing to adopt a family group of siblings, you will be welcomed with open arms' says Sarah Acheson, now deputy team leader with Family Placement Team at Bath and North East Somerset Council. She was our social worker when we adopted Clare.

Her view of the adoption process is that it should be 'as straightforward and transparent' as possible, with 'common sense' one of the primary factors in

approving parents and matching children.

'Adoption agencies are now in competition for adoptive parents and their guidelines are far less prescriptive than they used to be. There are no blanket bans.'

Few barriers

In the past, people who were very overweight were sometimes rejected as prospective adopters. Obesity is now considered a problem only to the extent it impacts on your ability to be a parent, and your longevity.

As to age, again there no blanket barriers – at 50 you could be fit, healthy and have a lot to offer. As a rule of thumb, there should be no more than, roughly, 45 years difference between your age and that of the child.

And you can be single, gay and from any ethnic background.

Odd man out

This is a key factor to consider when adopting:

Have you a child or children of your own? For the adopted child, getting on with birth children already well established in the family home might be a big problem, but it can be done. Agencies will help with training you in reassuring your birth child.

A plus of being childless is that you can concentrate on your adopted child, and he or she will not face problems arising from sibling competition or jealousy.

All about you

You're sure to wonder if you're suitable to adopt. You'll ask yourself if you are good enough. I know I did. I knew I was not the world's best housekeeper, and I knew my work was important to me.

It's OK to work – I made it plain I wanted to keep working, though as a writer I was able to work mostly from home. If you are part of a couple, then one of you (depending on the age of the child) needs to be at home more. Of course, if your child is at school, that can make work easier.

It's fine to not have a pristine house or be house-proud. I think it helps if you like cooking – but you don't have to! However, total chaos might not be the best thing.

Young or older?

You don't have to have a big garden, a small one, or even any garden.

You don't have to be young, although social workers want you to look ahead and be sensible – at 68, would you really want to be caring for a teenager?

Partnerships or singles, heterosexual or gay – it doesn't matter

Social workers don't insist any more on matching the child's ethnic origins. While a perfect fit might be ideal, there are other ways of matching, perhaps by finding a home for a child in an area with a substantial population with an Asian or West Indian background, even if the adoptive parents are not.

For example, most people in Bath and the villages around it are white, while Bristol has a large black community. A black child would be better matched in Bristol, where they wouldn't feel 'different' while in Somerset he or she might.

'No child will benefit from being the only black child in its neighbourhood – but it would be fine to have white parents and live in a community where there are other black children,' says social worker Sarah Acheson.

Emotional strength

The most important factor in managing this journey is your own emotional resilience. You need emotional stamina for sharing your feelings with other group members and with social workers (this could be a difficult step if you have never had any dealings with social workers), and you need emotional strength for the various ups and downs that will inevitably follow, even after the judge has signed the court order that makes the adoption final and irreversible.

As you progress, there will be uplifting times when it seems a child might be matched with you – and then you could be let down because circumstances over which you have no control have changed.

There are times when you can be close to despair and wondering why you embarked on this road – and other times when all seems to be going smoothly.

'The most important factor in managing this journey is your own emotional resilience.'

Going abroad

Unless your name is Madonna, adopting a child from abroad is a complicated and costly process. You have to pay for the cost of being assessed and approved, which could be up to £4,000. You still have to go through a local authority or voluntary agency and be approved by an adoption panel in Britain. Your application is then sent to a UK government department, which checks that your application meets the laws of the country you'd like to adopt a child from. Approximately 300 children every year are brought to the UK to live with adoptive parents. The first step is to think about which country you'd like to adopt from.

For more information, visit www.direct.gov.uk/en/Parents/ adoptionfosteringandchildrenincare

Case study

In Harrow, London, all children are matched within an average of six months, with the average waiting time of just four months. Harrow is in partnership with children's charity Coram. The government's adoption adviser in 2012 described Harrow's system as 'uplifting'.

Children in care go straight to the potential 'forever' family, which fosters them until they are able to adopt, instead of, as in the past, the child going to foster parents while waiting to be placed with adopters, and living with the foster carers while being matched.

Ethnicity is no longer a barrier. It shouldn't matter what race you are, and what race the child is, as long as there's a successful match, says Harrow.

Authorities have been firmly advised that instead of looking for 'the perfect family' they look for the best family available at that time. Harrow is one of the leaders in this, but there are many other agencies with the same strengths.

This is all good news if you've just started on the road to adoption!

Summing Up

▨ Take that first step – just starting on the journey will uplift you.

▨ Use BAAF's find-an-agency directory.

▨ Be aware the average age of adopted children is around four years.

▨ Most children in care are there because of serious neglect.

▨ You will need to be assessed and approved for adoption, which could take a year – but it's a far quicker and more straightforward process now.

▨ There are no blanket bans on types of people who are considered suitable.

Chapter Two

Early Days

You're in!

You've joined the pre-adoption group! After that first nervous plunge into a crowded room of prospective adopters is over, you'll feel much better. Each time you turn up, you recognise people and the atmosphere becomes more and more relaxed.

There's always an element of anticipation and, very probably, longing: everyone there is eager to share their home with a child.

This is an introductory information meeting which kicks off a four or six-week course, normally one evening each week. You get the chance to talk to guest speakers such as foster carers and parents who have adopted. This part of the process is extremely useful. It's a great opportunity to ask any questions and receive candid answers from parents who have actually adopted.

Social workers, despite their professional expertise, usually have not personally experienced adoption. People who have adopted can give you the most revealing and accurate idea of what awaits you.

No fails

At the first meeting there were the usual introductions, going round the group and we said, briefly, a little about ourselves – it was all very informal. As I recall, our group included teachers, a vicar and his wife, a couple with children of their own, a policeman and a school dinner lady.

'People who have adopted can give you the most revealing and accurate idea of what awaits you.'

It was stressed that no one would 'fail' this initial introductory course – but that those who felt it wasn't for them could of course leave the group. We had a presentation on adoption, and a little talk on the reasons why children might be in care. Refreshments were served: there was a pleasant atmosphere, though of course we were all a little nervous.

There were six of these meetings. Towards the end of the course, a social worker (there were two running the group) made an appointment to see us at home. For the most part, couples are seen together, but there are one or two sessions where the chat with the social worker is held separately.

Course content

These were the topics covered in the introductory course:

- Reasons children enter the care system.
- Legal adoption processes.
- Children's behaviour caused by neglect, abuse and malnutrition.
- Introduction to child development – both physical and emotional.
- How to meet and understand children's needs.
- The attachment process.
- Understanding the issues affecting adopted children and how they may feel.
- Settling children into a new home. (This is a popular topic and you'll be given heaps of help and information.)
- Contact with foster families, carers and birth family.
- Post-adoption support.
- Tips on how to get through the approval process. The main one was not to feel you are being judged – the social workers want you to be approved;

  they are not looking for ways to exclude you.

First visit

You will find that no matter how doubtful you were about joining a group, members do support each other. There's that 'We've all got to get through this – we're all in it together' feeling.

At the end of the course, a social worker from the adoption agency you're applying through will be assigned to come to your home and get to know you better – another hurdle you may not be thrilled by!

It felt very strange to even have a social worker coming to our house. But be welcoming to the social worker – the way you behave with her or him could be seen as typical of the way you react to everyone.

Your childhood

There are no intimate questions. You might be asked how you feel about being infertile or childless, but social workers don't dwell on this. I found the most intimate questions were those about my own upbringing. My experience is that almost everyone has criticisms of the way they were brought up!

Almost everyone feels their own parents were too harsh, had expectations that were far too high, and didn't love them enough. This was my feeling about my own parents. Yet the social worker is really just checking that you were brought up in a safe place, with no abuse or violence. I was properly cared for and looked after.

Why?

You will be asked exactly why you want to adopt. Be ready with an answer. If you've had IVF treatment, the adoption agency will need to be sure that you've properly grieved for unsuccessful IVF attempts and lost pregnancies. They may have a set period of time (six months to a year) that they want to have elapsed between your last IVF treatment and an application to adopt.

You may have altruistic reasons for wanting to adopt. If your lifestyle is comfortable and you have no money worries, you may feel you want to redistribute some of your wealth by giving a home to a child.

That's laudable, but remember that many children in care will have experienced multiple homes and have had a fragmented, tough life. So a child coming into your comfortable home might not necessarily appreciate this at once – and your pleasant lifestyle may be disrupted for a while. But this doesn't last forever; the rewards far outweigh the many conflicts!

Tidy up – a bit . . .

Tidy your home for social worker visits, but it doesn't have to look like an ideal home in a glossy magazine! One social worker told me that she feared the obsessively house-proud with a clinically neat house. How would such a household cope with a boisterous child? At the same time, total chaos might not be overimpressive.

Social workers do take a look round your house the first time they visit. They're interested in the room you've set aside for the adopted child – and of course your kitchen and bathroom should pass basic hygiene standards plus!

Talk tips

Advice from adoption social worker Sarah Acheson to prospective adopters going through the approval process and facing visits from social workers:

- Be straight – don't try to second guess.
- Don't downplay your vulnerabilities.
- Be honest.

She emphasises: 'Social workers are not there to catch you out – they want the process to work.'

Sarah believes these are the three qualities social workers look for in a potential adopter:

- Warmth.
- An open approach to life.
- Someone who can be thoughtful and reflective.

Pictures of you

As you move on with the visits, your social worker and the agency like to have copies of pictures of you and your home, pictures they can later pass on to children waiting for adoption.

Every member of your household is spoken to, so if you have other children or relatives living with you they can expect to be involved. Elderly people and children are treated gently.

The big question

Then comes the big question – have you anything in mind about the child you would like to adopt? I think it's best not to be too prescriptive. The more detailed your vision, the more warning signs the social worker might see. After all, you can't create your own birth child in exactly the design you'd like! But it's sensible to be clear on the kind of child you would definitely find difficult.

At first, I was adamant that we could give a home to a child – any child – in care who needed one . . . and that was that! But it was good that the social worker probed deeper. I really wasn't ready to consider a handicapped child, or one with serious behaviour problems, or a teenager.

It's not uncommon to have family groups, from twins to groups of four or five, available for adoption. A family group could be two, three or even four siblings – a wonderful ready-made family if you have the space or energy! There are never enough adopters for these groups of children.

Special gifts

Clare was from the group of children in care classed as 'special needs'. This was because of the years of grave neglect and ill-nourishment she'd endured. But special needs can also include special talents – the local authority will pay for any special lessons. The child does not have to be exceptionally gifted; showing unusual potential is enough.

Clare's foster parents had noticed her agility as she danced around their house. The local authority gave them an extra allowance for her to have weekly lessons at a local dance school. This included class fees and kit.

'It's not uncommon to have family groups, from twins to groups of four or five, available for adoption. There are never enough adopters for these groups of children.'

So 'special needs' can include special talents as well as disabilities. We continued with Clare's dance lessons, but she gave them up when she was 11 – much to my annoyance!

As an adoptive parent, you want to encourage your child in every possible way. When they give up interests for which they have an obvious talent, you'll be just like any parent: disappointed and a bit cross! But it might be an interest they resume years later: no life training is ever really wasted.

Clare still dances, but only at parties!

Enjoy your work

'You don't need to own your own home. But you do need to have the space for a new member of the family . . . and all of the toys and equipment.'

I made it clear from the start that, as a mum, I would definitely want to continue working. At that time, I was freelancing from home, but later I had part-time positions in publishing offices. When a child is at school, you have time for yourself to work if you wish. Our social workers never expressed any criticism; in fact they encouraged me.

It's more important that parents should be fulfilled and able to express themselves by working. To focus constantly on the adopted child – to have no other interests – might be counterproductive.

Full-time to flexible?

Can you go from full-time to part-time if you adopt? If you have worked more than 26 weeks for the same employer, you have the right to request flexible working arrangements. Your employer must consider the request fairly.

Once you are responsible for a child under six, or disabled child under 18, your employer is legally obliged to consider this. They can turn you down only if there is a good business reason.

You don't need to own your own home. But you do need to have the space for a new member of the family . . . and all of the toys and equipment.

Check and check again

You will need a Criminal Records Bureau (CRB) check, a full medical exam and report from your own GP, plus two references.

Who can be a referee?

■ Your GP.

■ A teacher who has been involved with your family.

■ Someone who has been your mentor, teacher or coach.

■ Your manager or boss at your place of employment.

■ A bank manager or other professional who knows you well.

Medical notes

The medical report is designed to make sure your health is up to the challenges of parenting a young child. The agency also looks at whether there are any medical conditions which could shorten your life expectancy. Your parents' health history will be considered, too. My husband thought this might be a problem, because at that stage he had not traced his birth mother and therefore knew nothing about his parents' medical history. It's a difficulty many adopted children have. It wasn't, though, an obstacle for us.

Ex-partners that you might have had birth children with are also contacted. This can cause awkwardness and a feeling of discomfort for you. But the main factor social workers want to establish is whether you have ever presented violent or aggressive behaviour. If you, your partner or a member of your household has ever been cautioned or convicted for an offence against a child, then the law will not allow you to adopt or foster children.

Fair report

The approval process can take up to eight months, with regular visits from your social worker, building up a picture of you. You see the report the social workers build up about you. It is possible to change parts of it. Since this is the report that will be given to the adoption panel, it's important that you feel it's fair.

You are able to see your home study report and its purpose is to demonstrate that you are suitable to adopt a child. The completed report goes to the agency's adoption panel – a mix which could include social workers, adoptive parents, adult adoptees, medical experts, teachers.

They consider the report and make their decision in private – you don't attend a meeting. They may have questions but these will go to your social worker. The panel decide if you are suitable, and also the age range and type of child they would be happy for you to adopt. Their findings then go to the senior manager at the adoption agency – and she will send you a letter confirming your approval. If you are declined – which occasionally happens – you have a right to appeal – visit www.irm-adoption.org.uk for details on how to do this.

'You see the report the social workers build up about you. It is possible to change parts of it. Since this is the report that will be given to the adoption panel, it's important that you feel it's fair.'

Timeline

Typical timeline of the adoption process:

1. You make initial contact with an adoption agency.

2. You go to an informal meeting held by the agency – a group meeting.

3. You attend a course of preparation and training in a group setting – four to six sessions.

4. First visit from a social worker to your home.

5. Police and medical checks. Referees.

6. Home study – when your social worker visits you over a period of a few months or longer. She completes your home study report, which goes to the agency's adoption panel.

7. Formal application sent to panel for you to be approved as an adopter.

8. The adoption panel looks at your application and the home study reports.

24

9. Official agency approval – you receive your letter! Celebrate!

Now the search to match you with a child begins.

Summing Up

- Show up at the pre-adoption course evenings – social workers do all they can to make you feel welcome.

- You don't need to be well-off or own your own home to adopt.

- Prepare ahead for the question: Why do you want to adopt?

- Be welcoming to your social worker; offer them tea or coffee.

- Special needs children may also have special gifts.

- You can still work and adopt a child.

Chapter Three

Approval

Search begins

You've been approved for adoption and you can now look forward to being a parent. The search is on!

While this can be a time of great anticipation for you, the attitude of some family members might surprise you: it can be less positive and helpful than you might expect. I was so aware of this possibility that I didn't say what we were doing until we were well down the line and at the matching point.

Even then, the response from family (except my grandmother) was unpromising. Apparently, I'd been pigeon-holed as the 'workaholic' and therefore wouldn't be that good as a mum! I also had a family reputation for being uninterested in housework and impractical.

So instead of cries of delight and encouragement, some of the reaction was negative. If this happens to you, try not to be upset. Other friends who had adopted told me of similar reactions. As soon as Clare arrived, the family couldn't wait to meet her and they loved her instantly.

Best friends

Friends were much warmer. The best friends I had, Judy and Andy, who had four young sons, were marvellously supportive. The first thing they did, when we were matched, was write a welcome letter to Clare with a picture of their family and pets, saying they hoped she could visit them soon, and how much she would enjoy her new home town.

'While this can be a time of great anticipation for you, the attitude of some family members might surprise you: it can be less positive and helpful than you might expect.'

Please, no advice!

Conversations about the adoption, while you are waiting, can become a little oppressive. People – however well-intentioned – ask why you haven't heard anything, and what's going on? All you can say is that you don't know, you're waiting . . . and try to change the subject.

When at last you are matched, friends might want to give 'advice'. You don't want 'advice' from anyone who has not been an adoptive parent or an adoption professional! I found it irritating when people warned me about how difficult it would be, how lonely Clare would feel being 'parted' from her mother, and how I must do this, that and the other. How would they know?

I think it's better not to reveal your plans until they are well underway – but that's just me. You may want to broadcast it, or just tell your inner circle. But be prepared to be constantly quizzed on progress.

Feelings matter

Your social worker makes regular visits,even when there's nothing new to report. They often ask you how you 'feel' at each stage of the process and that can be irritating – you always feel the same, just anxious to adopt a child. But it's best to come up with something to talk about rather than nothing. Make their visit pleasant. They've got a job to do!

Top tips

Here are my tips for the waiting period:

- Read all you can about adoption, especially attachment. There's a booklist at the end of this book.

- Put your notes into a folder and read through them. You should have built up some notes from the training course. The British Association for Adoption and Fostering (BAAF) has many publications, and you can subscribe to websites and newsletters, see the help list. I must admit that I should have studied more instead of focussing on getting a room ready and making plans. There's a tendency to keep thinking about the thrill of being a parent, rather than learning as much as you can about adopted children.

- Keep a diary if that's something you'd enjoy. A diary of your feelings as you wait to be matched is a kind of therapy.

- Don't put your life on hold. Still go away on holidays, keep working, and develop your other interests. If you close the rest of your life down, you'll spend all your time worrying and waiting. Only give up work – if that's your plan – when a child comes to live with you.

House move

We even moved house during the waiting period, as David was offered a job as editor of a daily newspaper at the other end of England. It was an offer he couldn't turn down. I let the new local authority and BAAF know that we were already approved for adoption and hoped to be matched – this doesn't happen automatically. We didn't have to go 'back to the beginning' of the approval process, but we did have to get to know our new social worker, Sarah.

Timeline lag

When the matching process begins, it is very easy to think the timeline is the same for everyone – you, the child, their foster carers and social workers. There's a tendency to think that everyone is working towards 'your' adoption at the same rate. In fact there may be many other issues for child, foster carers and social workers to deal with.

Rather than being two bits of a jigsaw, it's more that there are two jigsaws, yours and the child's, both being worked out, but not at the same rate.

Safe house

The child will still be coming to terms with having left his or her birth home. It may not be that long since they saw their birth mother. Clare has a distinct memory of being taken to see her mother for final meetings in a 'safe house'.

Clare was accompanied by her social worker, and parameters to which the birth mother would have to adhere would have been made clear before the meeting. These would include:

'Keep a diary if that's something you'd enjoy. A diary of your feelings as you wait to be matched is a kind of therapy.'

- Not giving the child false information – maybe by telling them they were going home.

- Not abusing the social workers or saying bad things about them to the child.

- Not harming the child, physically or verbally.

Safe times

Children will go to safe houses at a time that is sensitively arranged – not when they're just out of school and tired, not during school hours. Probably the meeting would be in a local authority children's centre with toys to play with. If the child is older, perhaps in a café. The meeting would be observed by social workers.

Foster family feelings

'Foster parents may have grown attached to the child; they might even have applied to adopt him or her, and if they'd been rejected, that could be a problem.'

Foster parents may have grown attached to the child; they might even have applied to adopt him or her, and if they've been rejected, that could be a problem. It was in our case. They will have to work through their emotions during the matching time. It's quite likely that the child will have grown attached to the foster family – Clare was with hers for two years.

Your child may have brothers and sisters who are also being adopted – Clare did. It was another issue for her to deal with, as they were all moving on. There's school and school friends – and pets – to say goodbye to. It's a very difficult time for the child. It's not a time of unmitigated joy. For everyone concerned in the match, there are different challenges at different times.

Waiting

As prospective adopters, we often think that the child is 'waiting' eagerly for a family with just the same hopes and expectations as we have. But that isn't so – their timeline is different. Their anxieties are different. Though their social worker will have told them she's looking carefully for a 'forever' family, the child's life is lived with the foster family. They can't really imagine a different life with any degree of reality.

Children's histories

Each child being released for adoption has a report, which if there's a possible match, you as a prospective parent can see. It contains information about the child, their birth family, an outline of their emotional and medical needs, and their present situation.

This gives you a detailed picture of the child that might be yours – and it's this report which makes difficult reading. It can be sad to learn of what the child has endured – at the same time, it's uplifting to think that you can make a huge difference to their life.

Health profile

The medical report on children released for adoption is detailed. It is done by a paediatrician and also looks at the birth mother's health during the pregnancy (including whether there was any known use of alcohol or drugs) and any known medical disorders in the birth family (including inherited conditions and genetic disorders). If known, there are details of the birth father's medical history.

Of course there are no guarantees that your child will remain healthy. There are no guarantees of that for any of us!

'It can be sad to learn of what the child has endured – at the same time, it's uplifting to think that you can make a huge difference to their life.'

Emotional challenge

It's the emotional challenges that will be harder to detect.

Children can appear to have one face when they're in foster care, or with a social worker, and quite a different one when they come to live with a 'forever' family. When they first arrive, there's a 'honeymoon' period. It's quite a shock when it comes to an end!

Foster parents and social workers may not have seen all the faces the child has. The official dossier isn't a picture that's complete.

'Foster parents and social workers may not have seen all the faces the child has. The official dossier isn't a picture that's complete.'

No judgement

When you have read the child's official report, you can decide whether to proceed. It won't be easy to say no, but you will not be judged if you do. We said no when we were 'offered' two children – siblings. We knew we wouldn't be able to look after two.

It's much better to say no at that point than move along with the process and then change your mind later. Trust your gut reaction.

Fair adoption

Adoption 'fairs' are held three times a year by local authority adoption agencies. Approved prospective parents are invited, and they can look at stands displaying details of children waiting for adoption and chat to the social workers.

False starts

As you wait, there may be false starts – we had three or four of them. Your social worker may outline details of a child, and he or she might sound just right for you. But at the next meeting this may have fallen through – perhaps the child was matched with a different family who had a little more – or something different – to offer that child in terms of life experience. It's no reflection on you!

False starts will depress you and at times you'll feel that there will never be a match. It's during the 'matching' period that you might begin to feel most disheartened. Just hang on to the fact you've been approved, have a lot to offer, and there will – eventually – be a match for you.

In my book, work is the great cure-all. Keep working, no matter what the work is. Practical work can be absorbing; I spent more time cleaning and de-cluttering than ever before. Meet trusted friends for drinks, go to the cinema, have a few days away if it's possible.

Wait over

We waited and waited. Then one day Sarah visited. When Clare's name was first mentioned and her details described to us, it took me by surprise. I'd decided to focus on other things than the adoption and suddenly – a possible match! My gut feeling was that this match would go ahead, and Clare would be ours. I had nothing to base that on except my intuition. But I was right.

Summing Up

- Family reactions to your news may be less than ideal – they'll change their tune when they meet your child.

- Don't put your life on hold as you wait – keep busy.

- While you wait, expect to have periods of despondency. Things will change.

- There are three adoption 'fairs' a year to which you will be invited.

- Some likely matches will fall through – no reflection on you.

- You will see a detailed report about a child the social worker wants you to consider – you can decide whether to proceed or not. Follow your gut instinct, and don't be afraid to say no.

- Trusted friends can support you . . . make the most of them!

Chapter Four

A Match at Last

A match . . .

Clare! We were to be matched with Clare, a seven-year-old girl born in Exeter and living with a foster family in a village near the city. I kept seeing her name everywhere – on T-shirts, key rings and coffee mugs.

This period was exciting; it was also more relaxed. If we were really going to meet her, I knew social workers were taking our match with her seriously, and that took some of the anxiety and tension out of the picture.

Careful steps

The matching process – before you meet the child – is done carefully. It's not quick. Once Sarah had told us about Clare – and we'd said we were interested – the next step was a meeting with Katherine, Clare's social worker.

She came for lunch and told us a lot about Clare. She'd been her social worker for years – Clare had been in and out of care and sometimes returned to her mother. She'd had three or four foster families. She'd been with the current one for more than two years, and was quite settled. They had a swimming pool and a pony. We didn't.

We gave Katherine some more pictures of us and our home. It was a good meeting. I could see that Katherine knew Clare very well. Her prime interest was whether Clare would be happy with us – not the other way round. Don't forget, there are two social workers you will get to know well. One is your own social worker, in our case Sarah, and the other the social worker for the child you're hoping to adopt.

'The matching process – before you meet the child – is done carefully. It's not quick.'

Meeting foster parents

The next meeting was with the foster parents, who had to travel to Bath from Exeter. Their views are taken into account – after all, they had cared lovingly for Clare.

This can be a difficult meeting for you, though not inevitably. If foster parents have formed a strong attachment to the child, they may be very involved. They may even have applied to adopt the child themselves (as happened with Clare) and been rejected. Would they try to raise objections to you? Would they throw spanners in the works to slow things down?

So, it's not the easiest of meetings. But, as Sarah says, it's vital that all procedures are transparent and open. The foster parents have a right to meet you and have their say.

'Be as welcoming to foster parents as to your social workers.'

Top tips

How to manage this first meeting? My tips:

- Be as welcoming to foster parents as to your social workers.
- Try to put yourself into foster parents' shoes – they face losing a child they and their family they have come to love.
- Don't try to impress them with the material goods or status you can offer.
- Say that if the adoption goes through, you'd like the child to retain links with them.
- Show an interest in their life, too, not only in the child – ask about their own children, interests and careers, and the area in which they live.

Honest answers . . .

They might quiz you on your plans for the child. They asked us, as a childless working couple, if we had many friends with children. Did we have much experience of small children?

Be truthful in your answers. I had only two friends – Judy and Andy – with children. My experience of small children was limited to playing with my sister's kids and some voluntary work with gypsy children many years earlier. No, it wasn't much experience. But how many couples expecting their first baby might say the same? Don't pretend because out of fear of getting a black mark. That won't happen. The more honest you are when hoping to adopt, the better.

. . . Tough questions

Other questions they might ask could be:

- What do you expect from this child? They might fear your expectations are too high.

- Do you realise how bad her background is?

- How will you cope with the child's adolescence?

- Do you mind your home being made untidy by a child?

- Do you realise that this cute little girl could turn into a difficult teenager . . . and a difficult woman?

- How much time would you have for her, since you're both working?

They love her, too

All these aspects will, of course, have been covered previously by social workers. They were happy with your answers. But if foster parents question you again, respond with humility and, crucially, honesty.

I don't think I put myself into their shoes enough. I don't think I had any idea how much they'd done for Clare and how they must have loved her. All I could think about was how we would love her, and what we could do for her.

The best thing is to emphasise that you understand it will be a long-term commitment, one involving hard work and very few expectations.

Timeline

Her birthday was in May and although we hadn't met, we were allowed to send her – via her social worker – a card and small gift. We met her in June. She came to live with us in September.

Here's our detailed timeline:

- Our social worker brought news of Clare.

- We met Clare's social worker at our home.

- We exchanged letters and pictures with Clare.

- We met the foster parents – they came to our house.

- We saw a DVD of her and her brother and sister playing with a social worker. I was a little uneasy about the DVD. I suppose in my heart I'd already adopted her and didn't like to think of 'my' child being videoed by social services, but I was quite happy to see pictures of her. Completely irrational! DVDs of children freed for adoption are no longer rare and are considered very helpful by adopters.

- Our first meeting with Clare.

- Second meeting: we took her out for the afternoon, with Katherine.

- We took her out for the day, with no social worker.

- She came to stay for one night . . .

- . . . then for a weekend . . .

- . . . and then for a week.

- She moved in with all her possessions, and started school locally.

She/he likes you?

You like the child, but he or she must also like you. If a child took a strong dislike to you, other visits would be arranged. But if still there was no chemistry between you, social workers will put the child's needs first, and the process would stop. This doesn't happen often.

Children of yours

Have you a child or children of your own? This could call for delicate negotiations!

Children already in the home – 'natural' children – will have to make adjustments, depending on their age and maturity. The newcomer child may seem like an interloper. The 'real' child might be jealous or resentful, unwilling to share toys and friends, or the two might just not get on . . . just like some natural siblings.

Rifts to come

None of this will come up in the honeymoon period of first getting to know the newbie. It's later on that problems might arise – and you as parents might start to feel that your own child's progress is being damaged by new family member. If your own child is clever and academic – and the new one isn't – there are more headaches. There will be differences in behaviour, vocabulary – and accents, perhaps – and eating patterns. Later, in teenage years, you can expect rifts and fallings out – but later still, if doors are kept open, things should be well again.

'Have you a child or children of your own? This could call for delicate negotiations!'

No address yet

All exchanges of letters are made via the social workers: it was quite a while before we had Clare's address. At the same time as we were told about her, she was told about us through her social worker.

It was several weeks before we first saw Clare.

Summing Up

▓ Matching is very carefully done and indicates you are being seriously considered.

▓ If the child's birthday is during the matching process, you should be able to send a card.

▓ You meet the child's social worker first.

▓ The meeting with the child's foster parents might not be easy – they love her too.

▓ The matching timeline is steady, gradually building up time spent with the child.

▓ You may not have the child's full address until your first meeting.

▓ Social workers support you every step of the way.

Chapter Five

First Times

First meeting

It's arrived – the day of your very first meeting with the child that's being matched with you. It's an incredibly exciting day, but also nerve-wracking.

I slept hardly at all the night before we met Clare.

You'll be the same. You will have seen pictures and maybe videos, exchanged brief letters. He or she will have seen pictures of you and talked about you to the social worker, who will have done much preparation.

Our social worker asked me to think about what I'd wear for this first meeting. You want to feel and look your best. I chose a soft cotton dress and bead necklace in the same vibrant turquoise blue – I felt bright colours would be right. You don't want anything too formal, too tight or too fashionable. You want to look like a mum on a day out with her child.

Test tea

It's likely that the first meeting will be centred on a meal, most probably tea at the foster home. Your child's social worker will be there too. It's courteous to take a small contribution to the tea – we took biscuits and cheese. For Clare, we took chocolate and a notebook with a picture of Bath on the cover.

Don't go overboard with gifts at this point; spoiling Clare later with too many presents was one of our mistakes!

'It's likely that the first meeting will be centred on a meal, most probably tea at the foster home. Your child's social worker will be there too.'

Nerves all round

Driving up to the foster home, set on a smallholding, I was nervous, and desperate to get a first glimpse of her. She ran down the lane to the car, smiled at us then ran back to her front door as, she later told us, she lost her nerve. Don't worry if the child shies away from you or retreats – they're anxious, too.

Of course, this isn't any ordinary tea party. There is ice to be broken – it can feel a little unreal. I can remember feeling jealous when Clare sat on her foster dad's lap and called him 'Daddy'. That was a bit painful, and unexpected. They weren't going to be her parents – we were! But foster children are encouraged to regard foster parents as Mum and Dad, and Clare had been in their home for two years.

This relationship with foster parents is delicate, especially so when their attachment to the child is obvious. Adoptive parents need to go carefully – you can't instantly be a family with your new child . . . it takes time.

At that first tea we talked about general subjects, including politics and local history, as adults do. Talking to the child all the time will put a strain on her. Of course, we asked her all the usual things – about her school, her pets' names, favourite foods and TV programmes.

Time alone

The tea was fine, strange but pleasant, and the foster parents encouraged Clare to show us her room and spend time with us in the garden on her own. It went all too quickly, and soon we were on our way back home.

Emotionally it was one of the most tiring days I have ever had. I was exhausted but happy.

Mention the A-word

We didn't mention adoption during the first meeting. I didn't want to frighten Clare by seeming to assume anything – after all it was her choice, too. But when the social worker saw us later to debrief us, she told us that Clare had been upset because we never mentioned it – she thought we didn't like her. My mistake again!

First day out

Because we hadn't been demonstrative enough to Clare, that first meeting was assessed as slightly unsatisfactory by Clare's social worker and foster family. But Clare had also said some positive things about us – mainly that she liked us, especially David, but she was not at all sure we liked her.

Naturally enough, we went overboard next time to show her we really wanted her. We visited a local tourist spot – a castle – and let her loose in the gift shop to choose things she wanted.

Go easy with gifts

She loved all the gifts, but the foster parents weren't too pleased, so once again we were in the doghouse. Warning – one small gift at a time!

It's hard, but restrain yourself and give presents modestly. Plan little games to play together. It was the first time she'd been in our car – and the first time the three of us had been together without the watchful gaze of social workers and foster parents – so we played a game (with small prizes from the bag of tiny gifts I had inevitably bought) trying to guess the colour of the next car we saw.

Get into a child's mind – don't treat them as an adult. There's a danger of doing that if you don't already have children.

'It's hard, but restrain yourself and give presents modestly.'

First weekend

Plan this weekend, but don't overplan. The one thing not to do is invite friends, relatives and neighbours to view your child! Much as you want them to meet your family and friends, save this for some way down the line. Instead, plan a simple weekend that's child-centred, making sure you have meals a child will like, some treats and maybe a children's DVD or two.

Mini-meals

If you do not have children of your own, the meals you plan might be a little too adult. I did roast chicken with all the trimmings, but this was perhaps a bit formal. Later on, I dished out fish fingers and burgers. If your menus don't include pizza, chips and milkshakes, now is the time to start getting used to them!

'Despite all the careful plans you've made for this first weekend, and all the treats you've prepared for your child, don't be surprised if they seem edgy or anxious.'

Be caring

Despite all the careful plans you've made for this first weekend, and all the treats you've prepared for your child, don't be surprised if they seem edgy or anxious.

I remember little Clare getting up several times during that first night, damping a tissue with cold water and pressing it to her head, explaining that she had a 'headache'.

She was reluctant for us to leave her when it was time for her to sleep.

Ordeal for her

I should have soft-pedalled my elation at her being with us.

For her, it was all a bit of an ordeal, though she tried her best to be as celebratory as we were.

It's amazing how small children in care are able to make this transition, to become someone else's child – not a situation they ever asked for or deserved.

Yet I didn't think of that so much then: my head was so full of excitement and joy that she was with us.

She comes to stay

At last she was coming to live with us! We drove down to Devon, met the social worker, picked Clare up and packed her luggage into the car. Loading her stuff into the car was emotional – this child had just seven bags of clothes and possessions – many of them second hand – to her name. She was leaving and really coming to live with us, to go to a new school and to start a brand new life.

I could see now that this was difficult for her. She began to cry. Don't be alarmed if he or she cries when they leave their foster parents – it's normal. Of course, you try to comfort them, but saying what a lovely time they'll have with you – which was what I did naturally, I so often put my foot in it – doesn't help them.

Let her cry

Instead, empathise and let them cry if they want. Once your child is back with you and her belongings unpacked, again a DVD and a nice meal will help. Too much conversation unsettles a child – children's films mean they can relax and not have to keep answering questions.

One of the first things Clare wanted to do when she'd moved in and all her things were stowed, was phone her foster mum. You must allow this. Her anxious 'How are you, Mummy?' was heartbreaking. Foster children are encouraged to call their foster parents Mum and Dad. You might wonder if you'll ever hold a central place in this child's affections. Don't worry, you will!

'You might wonder if you'll ever hold a central place in this child's affections. Don't worry, you will!'

Hide 'n' seek

The social workers suggested a week at home with me, then starting school, though this meant she started school term a week late. Clare settled in, seemingly radiant, but this period was a little artificial, I realised later. She loved to hide, wanting us to find her in the house several times a day. This got a little tedious after a while!

She would smile and laugh during the day, but I sometimes heard her crying at night – I tried to comfort her, but it's not easy. You do as much as you can, but it may be that your child needs to go through the pain.

We were now within reach of having Clare to be our daughter.

Summing Up

- Prepare for that very first meeting – you want to look and feel your best.

- Keep gifts to the child modest. Products from your own town or city go down well.

- Show the child your pleasure in them – they need to know you want to adopt them.

- Lower your expectations . . . expect good and bad emotions.

- See it from the foster family's viewpoint – they may have grown attached to the child.

- Don't be upset if child and foster family seem close and affectionate.

- Expect to feel drained and tired after the first meeting – don't plan anything for the evening.

- Debriefs might not be what you hoped for. Don't give up . . . keep going.

- Introduce family and friends gradually.

- Help the child fit into school – not stand out with expensive clothes or gadgets.

- Accept that friends may be hard to find at first.

- Be firm about house rules.

Chapter Six

Under Observation!

Observation

Clare moved in. We were a family. For the first year or so – until the day the judge signs the adoption order – you are officially foster parents. The good news is that you receive all of the fostering allowances, which can be generous. There's extra cash for birthdays and Christmas.

The not-so-good news is that there's a great deal of 'observation' and what may seem like invasion of your privacy for that first year. Social workers have to be 100 percent certain that all is going well, that your child is settling in and that you are feeling positive about the placement. And it's important that their checks are robust – they must see that the child is happy and thriving. Yet they are sensitive and they acknowledge that their 'observation' isn't easy for you. Visits can be as much as weekly to begin with, then fortnightly, then less frequently.

> 'There's a great deal of "observation" and what may seem like invasion of your privacy for that first year.'

Private chats

Besides visits from both social workers – yours and the child's – there may be visits from an educational psychologist. We had one visit from her, checking on Clare's progress with us and her attachment. Some of these visits will be with the child on their own, talking to them in their bedroom. This can feel uncomfortable – you don't know what they're saying about you! But it's fine. It's just to give the child freedom to speak openly.

You will probably have visits from your child's social worker – don't forget she is your child's link with the past. Make friends with her, be welcoming. It might seem to you that your child's social worker has a special relationship with her, because she will have known your child for longer than you have, and seen them through some incredibly hard times. Be grateful for this friendship: just look how much support she has given to your child.

Evening work

Sometimes the social worker will talk to the child separately, maybe just before bedtime and then come down and talk to you when the child is asleep. This can become very tiring – at the end of the day, all you want to do is rest and relax, have a drink, watch a DVD. Possibly your social worker does too – I don't suppose they welcome working in the evenings.

Besides these visits, there may be progress meetings at your house, attended by people from the local authority. It can seem that you're constantly tidying and preparing for visitors. Yet for me, after each meeting there was a sense of moving steadily on towards the goal.

'There's a precious scrapbook which is part of every child in care's luggage – the Life Story Book.'

The Life Story Book

There's a precious scrapbook which is part of every child in care's luggage – the Life Story Book. They carry this Life Story Book to each placement. The book contains a record of past and present and will contain their future.

The Life Story Book works with their memories.

The album may include drawings, poems, family trees, letters, bus and train tickets, photographs, writing and all sorts of ephemera that evoke the past, or provide clues to identity and individual histories.

Life stages

There will be pictures of your child's birth mother and family, their early home, pets, foster homes, first schooldays and later, of course, letters from you, and pictures of you. Each stage in the child's life is recorded, with the help of the child's social worker, working with sensitivity and empathy rather than sympathy.

When Clare first came to live with us and I saw her Life Story Book – which had been started when she was first in care – I admit it didn't make easy reading.

Early pictures

Depending on why the child was first placed in care, pictures of her birth home may show a certain amount of chaos and confusion. Clare's home seemed to be a sea of piled-up bags, junk and clothes, belongings strewn everywhere, no attempt at neatness . . . a life of disorder and neglect.

Some of the early pictures – when Clare and her siblings were first freed for adoption – showed a trio of children who were exceptionally thin and clearly malnourished, though smiling widely for the cameraman. You may have to steel yourself for these impressions . . . to the child, these pictures are precious.

And, despite all the problems with their birth families, there can still be love remaining, and often sorrow for the parents who treated them badly.

You'd be surprised how caring small children can be to mothers who have neglected them – and this is as it should be. If your child shows compassion, it's a tremendous sign. It means that, despite all they've suffered, their feelings are not so badly bruised that they no longer feel any emotion at all.

Showing these emotions is an excellent sign of psychological health.

Aide memoire

The Life Story Book can help a child to talk about losses, changes and separations and to remember the good things they've experienced too.

It's a positive project.

Family now

Having the child live with you is a huge thrill. If you were childless, you suddenly are a family: if you already have children, the new arrival fascinates all family members.

'If your child shows compassion, it's a tremendous sign. It means that, despite all they've suffered, their feelings are not so badly bruised that they no longer feel any emotion at all.'

Every minute was taken up: I had lots more practical work to do, and far less time for myself, but we loved spending time with her. Going shopping with her was a particular delight – buying her new clothes and toys, although buying a lot of new gear was not the best idea because she was really happy in her familiar clothes. Shopping was more a treat for me, really – showing her off and signalling to other mothers, yes, I'm a mum too!

Some breakdowns

There are adoption breakdowns: Adoption UK research suggests this could be as high as one in five. I felt terribly sorry for everyone involved when I heard a little boy near us was being sent back into care: his adoptive family had found him too demanding and there was friction between the boy and their birth daughter. This does happen. There's no blame, no judgement and social workers do all they can to help everyone through their distress and disappointment.

Visitors plus

So in that 'fostering' year there does seem to be a lot of intrusion – child psychologists, teachers, visits from foster parents and two lots of social workers – yours and the child's. You might visit the families of any siblings, and attend meetings for new adopters. You will be going to events at his or her school. There's endless support for any problems you may come up against.

Steel yourself for this first year of observation; it's not nearly as bad as it seems!

Settling your child in

The first year is one of the hardest – because, no matter what you've said or tried to feel, you do have expectations. Your child can be very sweet at first and it's a shock when they begin to behave badly.

They might challenge you, and be rude and demanding. But remember that all small children do this! It's vital not to let the child be 'in charge' – not for them to control you.

'The first year is one of the hardest – because, no matter what you've said or tried to feel, you do have expectations.'

Trial by telly

I was alarmed by the amount of television Clare watched; she seemed to be addicted to it. Since we watched very little, I found the constant noise and her sitting in front of the screen uncomfortable and worrying. She switched it on at every opportunity. When she started school, I limited it to two hours an evening, but she often crept down early in the morning to turn it on. Later on, her social worker asked gently if I would watch television sometimes with Clare. She said it would be bonding.

I started to watch *Neighbours* with her after school – and was surprised by how much I enjoyed it, and the shared experience of viewing together. I'd never watched daytime TV before.

David read her a story at bedtime, and I rented lots of 'good' children's DVDs. Her favourite was *The Little Mermaid*; she would want to watch it over and over again.

Tantrum time

Certain points were triggers for terrible tantrums: having a bath, washing hair, putting on warm clothes, getting ready to go out . . . she'd far rather stay in watching television!

I was surprised at this point when, no matter how badly Clare had behaved in private, she was able to behave well with visitors. She'd already picked up that 'smiling face' we all present to company, no matter that five minutes before we've been yelling at our family!

House rules rule

Expect this time of challenging behaviour after the honeymoon period. Your child might beg to go back to 'real Mum', even if there was a history of neglect or abuse, or back to the foster family. This will happen when they don't like your house rules!

A request for a gift or a demand to go home while you're on an outing together – just so that they can watch TV! – might mean your no is followed by sulks or tantrums.

Firm and fair

You must stick to the discipline and limits you wish to set. This was where I was really supported by social workers. They say it's critical for adoptive parents to be firm when it comes to behaviour and house rules. Don't give in just because you feel sorry for the child. Taking the easy way out at this stage – and it's very tempting to do that – will store up big problems later on.

One of the most difficult situations for parents to deal with is the disbelief of others outside the family who see only the child's endearing behaviour. These seem to belie the challenges exhibited in the home. My tip – don't even try to explain what happens at home to anyone who isn't an adoptive parent.

'Don't give in just because you feel sorry for the child. Taking the easy way out at this stage – and it's very tempting to do that – will store up big problems later on.'

Attachment

There is a lot more emphasis now on parents learning as much as possible about attachment problems. I know this was mentioned when we adopted Clare, but as a side issue. These days, potential adopters are encouraged to read as much as possible about attachment – it's the one thing you are most likely to come up against when you adopt a child. See my reading list at the end for some excellent books on this topic and chapter 8 contains more information on this issue.

Damaged trust

Reactive attachment disorder (RAD) is the result of developmental interruptions (often related to abuse and neglect) that generally occur within the first three years of a child's life. His or her ability to bond and trust (attach) to other people is damaged. Attaching to primary caregivers and others is non-existent, inappropriate, or negative, often involving violence in later years.

Brain waves

Understanding the child's attachment problems will help you so much in your adoption. The input of early experiences on the child's brain is seen as very important now. A child in care is likely to have had some extremely bad experiences – when they come to live with you in your loving and safe household, memories of these early experiences aren't just wiped out.

Memories

I think that when I had Clare, I did not take these bad memories into account often enough – I imagined that all the love and treats we gave her would make her happy and content. Sometimes they did, but there were still moments when although we might be having fun or on an outing, she would become sad and moody. I'm afraid I wasn't always as kind as I could have been. Now, I've learned a lot more about the brain. Clare wasn't able to instantly erase the memory of her real mother, or her foster family – and there's no reason why she should.

Distract!

My best tips:

- If your child acts up when a bath is on the agenda, or warm clothes are involved, just remember she was never exposed to warm baths or clothes when she was little. She was probably cold, hungry and neglected.

- Try distractions – bath toys, and novelty hats, scarves and gloves for going out. The fur 'animal' hats popular at the time of writing would have been ideal.

- If they become sad in the middle of a nice day out, be kind and empathetic without asking them to tell you what they're thinking. We're all sabotaged by our memories sometimes.

'Understanding the child's attachment problems will help you so much in your adoption.'

First day at school

Contact the local primary or junior school. They'll invite you to visit. The Head of our primary school was kind and welcoming to us, but warned us that Clare's start at school might not be easy. He had settled in children placed for adoption before, and was candid: there could be problems.

No mates

He was right! Small children can be suspicious of the stranger who has no 'real mum'. There will be many ways in which they can't share experiences. They won't have had many outings or any holidays abroad, or many new clothes or comforting toys gathered over the years.

Their vocabulary might be limited. And they will likely have had memories of being neglected or malnourished, which most of their classmates will thankfully never have had. No wonder, then, that they won't make instant friends, but will be looked on at first as a bit of an oddity . . . the odd boy or girl out, the one without a real mum.

'Contact the local primary or junior school. They'll invite you to visit.'

Not my mum

In your imagination, at the end of her first day at school you'll meet your child at the gates with a glow of pride. How lovely it will be when she rushes up to you and hugs you. Wrong again! Clare made faces at me as she walked down the path and would not acknowledge me – kind of embarrassing in front of other mums.

And this continued all the time she was at junior and secondary school – she never acknowledged me when we were at the school, or when she returned from a school trip. All the other kids rushed towards their mums while mine hid away!

Shabby chic best

Here's the big mistake I made for her first day at school – buying smart new trousers and tops when all the other kids were in practical, well-worn clothes. School uniform helps children to fit in. Kids can pick on those who are too well dressed. Just to reassure you – Clare now has an enviable and loyal group of firm friends she's known for years, some made at that first school.

Social worker Sarah confirmed that, in a time of dramatic change, children cling to what's familiar. It would have been better for Clare to wear some of the clothes she'd brought with her, clothes that were part of her. I realised all these things in hindsight!

Dance nerves

For a while Clare went to a dance school once a week and performed in some shows at the local theatre. But when it came to taking dance exams, she became very nervous and flunked out. This disappointed us and her teachers, who believed she had great talent and potential. But it's a mistake to force any child to do anything they are unhappy about. Her insecurities and lack of confidence were still with her.

Where's your real mum?

Gradually, she met family and friends, who loved her and were amazed by her, but her schoolmates were more cautious. 'Where's your real mum?' and (to us) 'Did you buy Clare?' were two questions I remember vividly.

Even when my little twin nephews, who were her age and pre-warned not to ask awkward questions, came to play, I overheard them quiz her. 'But what happened to your real mummy?' was a question she was unable to answer. I saw her hang her head in dejection. Best to just let this go and not intervene. Don't make a fuss; children say all sorts of things!

After a year, we were nearly at the adoption stage!

Summing Up

- You 'foster with a view to adoption' for the first year or so.
- Your child goes to a local school chosen by you.
- There are many visits from social workers.
- Expect challenging behaviour after a honeymoon period.
- Learn the triggers for tantrums – baths and warm clothes for Clare.
- Learn all you can about attachment problems.
- Class teachers can guide you in learning more about your child when she's not with you.
- Enjoy the new arrival!

Chapter Seven

Adoption Now

A-Day at last: Here comes the judge!

It had been one of the windiest nights of the year. Trees had been blown down, roads were littered with abandoned cars and the elderly had been advised not to go out. It was March, and cold.

Clare began this very special day by opening her gift, a silver locket, from David and I. She was nervous of what lay ahead – we tried to reassure her.

I'd hung a wreath of fresh pink and white flowers on the door, and we walked to the city centre, heads down against the storm. We sat in the waiting room at the county court . . . us, Clare and social workers, Sarah and Katherine.

The judge, driving in from the country, was delayed by the storm for about an hour – we waited anxiously. He arrived, waved hello to us and walked into his room to get ready. Soon we were ushered in. This was it!

Chocolate hello

The judge, wearing a plain black robe, welcomed us, and asked us all to give our names. On the table in front of him was a black box. He pointed to it and asked Clare to lift the box's lid. She was too nervous to so I did it for her. The judge put his hand in and brought out his wig, which was followed by bars of chocolate, which he gave to Clare. This delightful gesture set the mood. Clare began to relax.

My memory of the hearing was that it was over in a flash. Neither David nor I can remember what the judge said. We assume he must have asked us – and Clare – if we were happy for the adoption to be made legal and binding, and that he signed the court order.

We went from the court to the Pump Room, where I'd booked a table for a celebration breakfast – croissants, coffee and a glass of champagne for the adults, juice and a sandwich for Clare. Outside, gale force winds were shaking the town! Clare went back to school, and the rest of us returned to work – with a slight feeling of anticlimax. Was that it?

The other hearing

The birth parents are always invited to a legal hearing some weeks before the judge signs the papers. Adoptive parents do not attend this one. Birth parents are given the opportunity to give their comments.

'The birth parents are always invited to a legal hearing some weeks before the judge signs the papers. Adoptive parents do not attend this one.'

They might say they don't want their child to be adopted, or they might say they agree. Their statements are recorded, but whatever they say cannot change the outcome. It's for the record, making the process transparent and evidenced.

The judge, on the advice of social workers, has already decided that the adoption should go ahead. Social workers tell me that most birth parents do not take up the invitation to attend this hearing.

Family and friends!

More celebration followed. Family members bought gifts and cards for Clare and we had a tea. Friends, too, wanted to celebrate her adoption, so we went out for dinner. Perhaps we went a bit over the top with our festivities. Too much celebration might be a bit bewildering for the child, who, after all, has only been with you for a year or so. We were still in the stage of honeymoon really – and still wasting money on 'stuff' to celebrate!

Same same!

The actual adoption – sealed by the court order – doesn't make an instant difference to the family. This was another error of mine: I imagined that once it was a reality, everything would be 'alright'. In fact, some behaviour problems continued. Perhaps the parents benefit from the adoption hearing more than the child. For them things haven't really altered.

Start of love

I always remember something a social worker told me during the adoption preparation – that the start of love emerges only after two years of a family relationship. I think this is true. Until then, there's a kind of fantasy.

Of course there is love, but not the deep unshakeable love you get when links have been forged never to be broken. This is the unconditional love – the one that never ends!

Discipline

Discipline is the hardest responsibility of parenthood. With an adopted child, it's even more difficult – it feels like disloyalty when you have to be tough with the child you've waited so long for. You feel mean when you have to refuse a request or insist on better behaviour. Yet the child must fit into your life – not the other way round.

I recall one social worker telling me the child must bend to our house rules and our judgement. At the time, I thought this was harsh. But it's absolutely right – you don't want to alter your life to tie in with the child's demands. It is possible to change a child's values for the better, even at what seems a late stage in their lives. It's just that it won't happen overnight.

Find friends

Don't make a big deal about adoption where other kids are concerned. If they've met Clare at school, they don't need to understand what adoption is and why she was adopted. All that matters is that they are friends.

Don't be alarmed if your adopted child still has trouble making friends. They might:

- Put friends off by seeming 'different' to them in some indefinable way – that's until they get to know them. Let other children get used to them.

- Not have the vocabulary they do. Ordinary words such as mortgage, hotel, dessert, cash machine, two-for-one and many others are part of the landscape for most families. Not for the child brought up in neglect. The

'Discipline is the hardest responsibility of parenthood. With an adopted child, it's even more difficult – it feels like disloyalty when you have to be tough with the child you've waited so long for.'

adopted child might never have come across them. In any case, their vocabulary – their list of words – will likely be much shorter than those of her school mates. Their early years won't have included much in the way of verbal communication.

- Be so addicted to television that this will put off normal children – even if they're quite keen on television themselves. Lively small children do want to play outside and try new activities. Your adopted child might just want to sit in and watch TV all the time, even on the sunniest of days. I heard one of Clare's friends mutter, 'It's boring that you just watch television all the time! Why don't we play outside?'

Careful with cash

Remember that once the adoption takes place, most of the financial benefits dry up! Of course you get Child Benefit, but the generous fostering allowances stop. This is when you can begin to feel less well off especially if, like me, you tended to spoil your child.

Paid parenting

'If you are employed and adopt a child, you may be entitled to up to 52 weeks of adoption leave – but only one member of a couple can take it, so if you are both working you need to choose.'

If you are employed and adopt a child, you may be entitled to up to 52 weeks of adoption leave – but only one member of a couple can take it, so if you are both working you need to choose. Adoptive fathers could be entitled to a short period of paid paternity leave. Statutory Adoption Pay is paid for a maximum of 26 weeks.

Budget boost

Save cash by:

- Working out what your budget will be after the adoption cash dries up – and try to live within the budget before it does. Perhaps you could save even half of the allowances? You could put them into an account for holidays and travel, or put some of it into an account for your child. It's much later – maybe when she's setting up home or trying to budget in her first job, or running up credit card debts – that she'll really welcome your bail-out cash.

- Trying to reduce treats and gifts. Here's a marvellous tip – children love new things, but they don't have to be brand new! Charity and vintage shops sell toys and games at knock-down prices, and so does Amazon. I wouldn't, though, buy second-hand clothes for your child unless he or she likes them. Clare had been so used to hand-me-downs that she loved having new clothes. Just go for inexpensive ones.

- Trying to soft pedal that feeling that your adopted child must have 'only the best'. Keep pocket money in line with what their friends get. Instead of purchasing all the latest fads which they might not use, give some vouchers as gifts.

Which school?

Think about your child's education. In my opinion, state primary and junior schools are excellent; it's at the secondary stage that you might want to think about private schools. Yes, it's expensive, but there are 'small schools' and charity-run schools which offer the special attention and care that might be needed by a boy or girl whose early years of education – in school and at home – were disrupted or even negligible.

Needless worry

But I think parents worry too much about education. Unless your child is highly academic or exceptionally gifted, practical and social tools – and good manners – are the skills to encourage. They take a child a long way.

It's at the college or university stage that there are real choices to be made. Clare wanted to leave her private school early – she gained 7 GCSEs – to join a fashion course at the city college. After this she went full-time at Dolcis where she'd been a Saturday girl and then she joined Top Shop, where she has progressed up the management ladder.

Let an adopted child make their own career decisions.

'Let an adopted child make their own career decisions.'

First holidays together

Taking your adopted child with you on holiday is fabulous. You are introducing them to new experiences. Make the first holidays as simple and stress-free as you can – avoid complicated or excessively long journeys.

Sand and sun probably wins over the city holiday. Clare loved Greece. We went several times. She built a friendship with a local Greek child, one which lasted several years. She learned to snorkel. She learned a little easy Greek.

A weekend in London was very successful, and so easy to arrange. Clare enjoyed seeing Starlight Express in London and going to The Hard Rock café for a burger. At home, she always enjoyed going to Sainsbury's and frequent visits to the garden centre's pet department. As always, the simplest treats were usually the most successful! I wish I'd done more of them.

Reconciliation

Your child is still settling in. They're doing their utmost to reconcile their past and their present – and doing well. Now and again there are problems, but the general picture is one of slow but steady progress.

So you've adopted, they're yours – no more visits from social workers . . . but you've only just begun.

Summing Up

- Enjoy the adoption day – have a little celebration. It's nice to have flowers in there somewhere! Give your child a little gift.

- Birth parents are invited to a separate hearing some weeks before. Their views on the adoption are recorded for posterity.

- No instant difference is created by the adoption ceremony!

- Disciplining your child is the hardest responsibility – but it must be done.

- Don't worry if other children are wary of your child. This vanishes in time.

- Paid adoption leave is on offer for one parent.

- Plan holidays and days out that are simple and stress-free.

Chapter Eight

Ours At Last!

At long last, Clare was our own child. The social worker visits – the checks, the assessments, the progress reports – were over. No one but us was involved with her upbringing. Once your child is legally yours, your responsibilities are the same as any other parent. Celebrate! You've adopted, you're now a parent and you now have a family!

It's a fantastic feeling. I was very proud of Clare. I loved going out with her; taking her to different places, and arranging parties for her.

There were still difficult times when she wouldn't talk to us and never expressed any physical warmth – no cuddles, no holding hands. This was a hard time. Often when we were out, she would relapse into kind of gloom just at the moment when I thought she'd be happy and excited.

This was tough. I didn't cope very well. Often I'd be cross, puzzled as to why she was behaving like this. But she wasn't behaving badly at all – she just wasn't being warm and demonstrative.

Hide away

If we went on a canal walk together, she'd lag behind me and then keep hiding, constantly dodging behind a tree when I looked round. This was fine behaviour for a five-year-old, but not perhaps for a girl of her age.

I suppose my main 'complaint' was that she wasn't like my friends' children – but why should she be? She'd come from a different place.

But one of my happiest memories is putting her to bed after a long, sunny and contented day. 'I like it here now,' she murmured just before she went to sleep. That was one of the happiest moments of my life!

The expectations trap

The main trap in adoption is to have expectations – that your child will be this or that, will excel, and will follow to the letter all the advice you give.

This is the thing: in today's world, we can't direct our children's lives. We can't make them take one route or another; we can give only guidance and support. There's a danger with adopted children of wanting them to exceed, wanting them to show visible signs of how well they've done, how they've triumphed over their own initial damaging circumstances.

You can fall into the trap of being overambitious. It's best to steer with a light touch, to relax and let the child step out into adulthood. My feeling was that it might be when she was 30 or even 40 that Clare could need us most emotionally, not when she was a little girl and still growing up.

'There's a danger with adopted children of wanting them to exceed, wanting them to show visible signs of how well they've done, how they've triumphed over their own initial damaging circumstances.'

Look after yourself

When you adopt, do not give up on being you – or on looking after yourself. Adoption isn't for the faint-hearted, so you need to keep re-enforcing your own strength. This could mean anything from yoga to zumba classes and all the things that make you feel good – hairdressing appointments, aromatherapy, seeing friends in wine bars, cinema and workshops – anything that gives you energy and makes you happy.

Don't be an adoption bore!

Adoption can cause distress if it's the only thing you think and talk about. I was guilty of that from time to time; I'm sure I became an adoption bore. I was especially anxious when we were in company, worrying about Clare far too much and 'checking' on her too often. I didn't know how resilient children are!

You need friends

Use your support network of friends and family – and make sure you stay in touch with the grown-up world you've been used to. We hadn't bargained for the extra costs of going out, since we had to have – surprise, surprise, a babysitter. What I'd do now is join a neighbourhood rota of babysitters . . . or perhaps it can be less stressful to just hire a new DVD and buy a bottle of wine!

Cash

The allowances you had during the fostering period in the run-up to the formal adoption stop, but you start to receive Child Benefit, a weekly allowance paid straight into your bank account. At the time of writing, it's £20.30 a week for your eldest child and £13.40 a week for other children.

Stay in touch!

Should you keep in touch with the social workers now you don't have to? Some parents breathe a sigh of relief and wave them farewell when the adoption papers are signed. I can understand this, but we chose to keep in touch with Clare's own social worker, Katherine, and she made several visits to us over the years, when she was in Bath. She came for tea and a catch up. She had known Clare the longest, and seen her, lovingly, through bad times.

We also kept in touch for a while with Clare's delightful 'foster-sister', Zoe, the daughter of her foster family. She also came to visit. I think it's good to hang on to these links . . . these friends are part of your child's history.

Relationship problems

Your adopted child might seem to have more problems than 'normal' children in making relationships. They may idealise best friends, or tend to fall out with friends for no reason. This means they may have some bewildered friends!

Often, he or she might think they're being rejected by children who are doing nothing of the sort. Yet once a strong friendship has been forged, these can be enduring. Clare, now in her 30s, has close friends she made at the local school when she was ten.

Keep on helping and supporting – this never stops.

Attachment disorder

Adoptive parents are encouraged to read up all they can on attachment disorder. I am sure Clare had a form of this.

It can be a by-product of adoption and happens because simple things such as being picked up when they cried as a baby, or taken out to places holding hands, were never experienced by the child.

'Adoptive parents are encouraged to read up all they can on attachment disorder.'

The attachment that happens between parent and child is usually an instinctive and natural thing. It helps a child to develop the all-important boundaries, emotions and ways of communicating. When that bond and experience has been disrupted in some way – either through neglect, abuse or loss – the child's development will have been affected. It's almost impossible that any child could go through abuse and neglect without being damaged.

Not you

Be prepared for challenging and upsetting behaviour. As an adoptive parent, do not think it's because of something you've done, or not done. It's not directed at you, though it seems that way.

A secure attachment means that a child doesn't want their parents to leave and will be comforted when they return. With attachment disorder, this simple equation breaks down. These are the main problems:

- Avoidant attachment: A child shows no distress at the parent leaving and no tangible response when the parent returns.

- Ambivalent attachment: This is very confusing. A child shows distress when a parent leaves, but is willing to be comforted by a stranger, and then shows a reluctance to warm to the returning parent. It can be very upsetting.

- Disorganised attachment: A child will struggle to adapt to a parent's return and may start to 'freeze'. Attachment disorder children can switch between being menacing and charming. They can offer angry and threatening behaviour, often avoiding intimacy and close relationships, or switching between behaviours.

Symptoms

Symptoms may range from mild to severe – with mild being something you can't distinguish from those of a normal naughty child. Clare had a mild version, but here's the full symptoms checklist:

- Problems in social situations, with difficulty in smiling or making friends, over-controlling behaviour. This can alarm other little children and make it hard for your adopted child to find good friends at first.

- Emotional problems such as lack of empathy, affection with strangers, angry outbursts and severe and extended tantrums.

- Long crying fits.

- Anger and aggression aimed at carers, especially adoptive mothers: refusal to accept any blame, breaking possessions, forcing conflicts.

- Developmental problems can include poor hygiene and deficient awareness of danger, hoarding food or gorging on it. Some children appear to have no conscience, and their morals – their sense of right and wrong – might be confused.

Fade away

By no means will you have to face all these difficulties. We certainly didn't.

These are all challenges that can fade away. Your social worker will help you enormously, reassuring and helping you to put things in perspective. The good bits far outweigh the bad!

Look to the future

If you can look ahead, your adopted child will likely lean on you for support when they're in their 30s rather than when they're a little girl or boy. Keep the future in mind. Expect that all will be well.

Keep celebrating!

Continue to celebrate the adoption, perhaps with a tiny gift, a card or a meal out. We did this for the first few years, then it fell away. We are now planning a 20-year anniversary – a restaurant meal with Clare's brother and his adoptive parents.

Summing Up

- Do use post-adoption support networks – see the reading list at end of the book.

- Prepare for some form of attachment disorder – read all you can about it.

- Keep in touch with favourite social workers.

- Look after yourself!

- Hang on to mementoes of their upbringing.

- Celebrate the adoption all over again – a dinner or party, a small gift.

Chapter Nine

Turbulent Times

Hard times, good times

The teenage years with your adopted child will be a trial - just as they can be with any teenager, adopted or not. The cheerful, chatty ten-year-old changes into a moody, monosyllabic fourteen-year-old – and suddenly all the pleasure and fun you shared together seems at an end.

No more laughs, no singing or dancing, no enjoyment for your family and friends because she doesn't want to see or speak to them – or you – now.

Moody blues

In Clare's case, the moody years seemed to last forever, at least until she left home. Her bedroom at the top of the house became her refuge in which she watched television, had all of her meals and even put up her own Christmas tree.

She never shared a meal with us. She did her own laundry, cooked her own food or ordered takeaways, and talked to us very rarely. Friends who came to stay were amazed at my 'ghost' daughter who never put in an appearance, not even to say hello.

It was embarrassing when they talked about their own children, and when I met their well-mannered offspring – yet at the same time, Clare was law-abiding and hard-working . . . and silent, at least to us.

When we did exchange words, it invariably ended up in full-scale rows as she refused to have anything to do with the running of the house. Even small things such as shopping and helping with cleaning were refused.

> 'The teenage years with your adopted child will be a trial – just as they can be with any teenager, adopted or not.'

Locked out

I was very angry when a dance teacher came to stay with us. She was giving a late class and a performance, so I gave her a key to the house and asked Clare several times not to lock the door when she came in. But she did lock it, so I had to get up at two in the morning to let in a guest who was alarmed when the door wouldn't open. Clare did not apologise.

School trips and days out were a problem. When meeting Clare, she would not acknowledge me. She'd walk gloomily to the car. She was always the very last child to come out of her class, so I was always waiting a long time.

Dealing with traumas

I think Clare had decided to recognise us only as sponsors, not as parents. She tried as much as possible to lead her own life, treating her bedroom as a flat within the house and having minimal contact with us.

She worked very hard at school and at her Saturday job, and was always punctual and well dressed. She did all her own laundry from the age of 12. I hadn't asked her to; she just didn't want contact with me.

What had we to complain about? She didn't take drugs or drink, wasn't wild, worked hard and did her own washing and catering. Yet there was a sense of misery, for me, at being so ignored from the life of the child I'd taken such delight in adopting and looking after.

Poor eating

Since she refused to eat with us, Clare's diet became very poor. She had a Saturday job in a shoe shop – plus pocket money – and usually spent this on food, always pizzas, which she had delivered to the house by herself. She never shared them.

Leave her alone

I went to see a therapist when things between Clare and I got unbearably bad, and she 'wouldn't do' all the things I wanted her to do. For example, I would have liked her to continue her schooling rather than leave after GCSEs. She wanted to leave and start work.

His advice was simple: 'Leave her alone. Let her make her own decisions.' He was right. Clare decided to take a fashion and textiles course at the city college, and this proved to be a good foundation for her career in fashion retail.

If your adopted teenager won't talk to you or recognise your household, leave it be . . . learn to live with it. Continue to be there when needed, always be pleasant, and make sure they have all the things they need, even if they won't ask you to shop for them.

As long as they are safe, well and meeting their own work timetable, live with that. I know it's easier said than done!

Christmas – far from happy

Christmas was often a bad time. After the cosy years as a little girl, Christmas Day was usually a nightmare of sulks and unpleasant behaviour. Your child may rip all the wrappings off gifts frantically in an effort to find a 'better' present. It's horrible to watch!

Birthdays, too, can be times of trial. Clare did not want to celebrate with us, but we did give her the gifts she requested. She would seem sad and moody on her birthday, retreating to be by herself. Looking back, it's hard to reconcile the difficult teenager with the delightful girl she is now.

Do not despair. Remember too that all teenage years are difficult, and not just for adopted children.

'If your adopted teenager won't talk to you or recognise your household, leave it be . . . learn to live with it.'

Swap notes

Share notes with friends who also have adopted children. Whatever seems outrageous and awful now will be part of the past in a few years as your teenage child grows into adulthood.

Overreaction?

You might find that the adopted child's fidelity to boyfriends and girlfriends is very strong, and that when there are break-ups their long-lasting distress and sorrow may seem like an intense overreaction. This is where you can really help . . . just by listening and offering comfort.

Safety first

'Share notes
with friends
who also
have adopted
children.'

Contraception and health – give advice when it's asked but, again, don't interfere. My feeling is that a teenager's love life is their own business, provided they're aware of safety precautions and the consequences of ignoring them.

Career plans

This really is a decision best taken by the child, based if possible on your advice. Clare's decision to leave school after GCSEs and do a fashion course at the local city college was the right one. I think every parent can become too involved with their child's education and money can be wasted.

Also, it's unwise to imagine that a child's entire career can be mapped out at 16. A few years on, the landscape might have changed completely. I've known many parents who had great plans for their children, only to see them dashed. Instead of appreciating their child's achievements, they instead felt let down.

Encourage work

This is my advice: curb your expectations. To have a healthy, happy, independent child who can support themselves – that's quite a high aim these days.

I think the work ethic – not something always nourished by schools and universities – is just as important as a formal education. Your adopted child can take a Saturday job and holiday jobs, it's all to the good. Shop work, café work . . . anything entailing dealing with other people, meeting deadlines and goals, and working for their living.

Fill the gap

There are few rewards during this patch. All the progress you've made with your child might seem in vain. For us, it was as though Clare had 'divorced' us for several years. It's especially painful if you see your child eating badly and not looking after themselves – such a contrast to the lively little thing you cared for so well.

New interests

This is the time to keep an eye on your child, avoid engaging them in questions about their behaviour . . . and develop new interests for yourself. During the little girl years, Clare was my main interest, although I was working as a freelance writer.

I realised that life as a mum to a little girl had been very time-consuming, even though that's what I'd wanted. There was always something to do. Even the practical things – shopping, laundry, cooking, ferrying her around – were enjoyable. I especially liked doing meals for us, and going shopping with her for clothes. But it was all over now!

Engage in life

I found I had a gap to be filled when she'd retreated from us, otherwise I could waste time thinking and being sad about the past, the little girl who had vanished. I took on extra work, did courses and made more friends.

There are so many courses you can take. If you haven't been working, now might be the time to look for part-time job. Look for something that really absorbs you. Yoga and pilates are good for relaxation, although you don't get to know as many people as you would at a more 'sociable' class.

I think paid work is the best thing: there's nothing like the company of other people, office banter and after-work drinks to help you disengage from the trials of your teenage terror.

Support is there

There is post-adoption support! There are groups you can join and sites you can subscribe to online. You have only to contact your adoption agency to find the nearest post-adoption support group.

'Never give up on your child. No matter how bitter the words hurled during a row, keep that door always open – and make sure your child knows your support and your love is forever.'

You don't have to feel you are battling alone. Your child isn't the only one who is hard to manage. Many adoptive parents will commiserate with you. Parents of birth children, too, complain about the teenage years. It's not unique punishment for adoptive parents.

Hang on to the thought that, if you get through this, it will be all change in a few years' time, as it surely was with Clare. Never give up on your child. No matter how bitter the words hurled during a row, keep that door always open – and make sure your child knows your support and your love is forever.

Summing Up

- Prepare for the teenage years to be turbulent – they are with all children, not just adopted ones.

- Don't have any expectations regarding careers or education successes. Celebrate whatever is good, no matter how modest.

- Don't try to map out a career and life plan for your adopted child. Too many parents do this.

- Never compare your child with friends' children.

- Encourage paid work in any form – a Saturday job, holiday jobs, washing dishes or serving burgers. Rather than working for you at home, encourage your child to get a job in a shop, café, fast food bar etc.

- Don't interfere in your child's romantic life, but give advice if it's asked for. Safety is paramount – mention that your GP can always see them confidentially. Provide a relaxed – not a critical or strict – environment.

- If your adopted child tries to turn their bedroom into a flat and becomes a recluse, live with it. It can be a prelude to moving out of the parental home.

- When your child makes firm plans to move out, don't be resentful – be encouraging. Independent living is good. Maybe their first step will be living with a boyfriend or with another friend, or on their own.

- Make sure your child knows you are always on hand for help and advice. I would add 'and cash' – that's a given, even though you'd prefer to hang on to your money!

- Always keep the door open. No matter how bitter the fight, how seemingly final the words hurled in anger, never give up. Make a habit of reconciliation. Then your child will know that you'll never desert them or stop loving them, no matter what. That's what parents – adoptive or not – do.

Chapter Ten

They're 18!

Your child is now 18 . . . and can legally contact birth family. This could mean getting in touch with a mother who neglected or maltreated them, with parents who were feckless. They will have been legally removed from them, and all these years they have been banned by law from making contact with them.

How will you all cope?

Records

You will have kept your child's records, the official account of how they came to be in care. This details their birth, how they were treated as a child, any police involvement with the family and usually some details of the birth parents and their background, with medical information.

It will also describe his or her progress with different foster families and social workers. It can be a sad read.

Her right

Clare had a steady boyfriend when she was 18, and they were looking for a flat together. Her view of us had mellowed . . . a little!

She wanted to read her reports, and she had every right to do so. I think most adopted children, once they are grown up, would find the reports impossible to ignore. They'll be curious, some more so than others.

Sit with her

We sat with her while she read them: she was nervous, yet excited. Do sit with your adopted child at this time, if he or she lets you.

This window into your early life must be compelling – I can understand any adopted child wanting to read the reports. They'll be looking for answers. They'll want to know what their birth mother was like, and perhaps they'll also want to know what happened to her after the adoption.

They will probably be far less curious about their birth father. Research shows that most of the adopted children who try to locate their birth parents start their search with the mother in mind.

'I can understand any adopted child wanting to read the reports. They'll be looking for answers.'

Hang on to reports

Despite the possible urge to destroy them, I would advise parents to hang on to these reports. They are not graphic. They are written by social workers giving their observations.

It will seem strange to think that your much-loved child was once this waif without a proper home, 'in care'.

Letter to go

Clare was upset by the reports, yet thanked us for showing them to her. She decided to write a letter to her birth mother: the address was easy for her to get, from an older brother who had got in touch with their mother.

This was a strange time, but I wasn't upset by her decision at all. Part of me was curious: how would this woman, who had all her five children taken into care because of serious neglect, have fared over the years? I had read notes on her own background as a child – and that was saddening, too. I felt some compassion: the whole situation was unhappy.

Despite the awfulness of early reports about Clare, there were still times when I felt sorry for her mother – sad that any mother could come to such a pass. One of the things that distressed me was the lack of food Clare had been given, and the surprise with which she first greeted our full larder and fridge.

'There's always lots of food here,' I heard her telling a friend. It's words like these which threaten to undo you and make the adoption process so intense.

Travelling girl

I did not ask to see the letter Clare wrote to her birth mother, but she showed it to me anyway. I was warmed by the fact that she told her she was happy with us, and had been . . .

' . . . brought up travelling . . . I have visited Greece several times, and France, Spain, Wales, Venice, and a school ski trip to Austria'.

She outlined some of the things she'd done, and mentioned the fashion course she was just finishing. She wished her mother well.

Letter back

A letter came back very swiftly, enclosing a photo of her mother with a man who was now husband, on a holiday in Spain. It was encouraging to see that her mum had made a life for herself – she looked so much better than in the early pictures I'd seen. She said she hoped to see Clare again.

Flashbacks

Clare decided not to write again to her mother; she didn't explain why. It's possible that she might change her mind later on. Be aware that this might happen with any adopted child, at any age.

For several years now – and she's over 30 – she has expressed much anger towards her birth mother and says she is sometimes troubled by 'flashbacks' of early life. All you can do is listen and give comfort – as always.

He was adopted too

We had encouraged Clare to contact her real mother, if that is what she wanted to do. David was adopted himself, at birth. His mother had been a refugee, living in London, from Nazi-occupied Austria. He was brought up happily by a couple living in a one-bed flat. His adoptive father was a warehouseman.

After both his adoptive parents had died – and after he felt Clare felt settled with us – he decided to search for his real mother. After 18 months, he traced her to a flat in North London where, after some initial anxiety, she agreed to meet him.

They formed an affinity and, until she died, met often. David found he had an uncle and a half-brother, too. These experiences helped Clare.

She met Greta, David's real mother. 'A survivor' . . . was the expression Clare used to describe her first impression of Greta.

'When your child, at 18 or later, decides to contact his or her birth mother, this might be a time when you need extra support.'

Strong bond

An educational psychologist had predicted in the very early pre-adoption days that Clare would form an exceptionally strong bond with David, and this proved to be the case.

While Clare and I had many squabbles and fights, Clare and David never did! In fact he often had to referee our fights. There were many times when I seemed to run out of both energy and patience at the same time, which is when you are most likely to experience conflict with your child.

Call in support

When your child, at 18 or later, decides to contact his or her birth mother, this might be a time when you need extra support. Maybe your child will decide to make a visit to her.

It might be a troubling time for you, and you should contact either the local authority family services division, or the independent agency who arranged the adoption.

Post-adoption support varies across the country, but most agencies now have a post-adoption worker. It's recognised to day that there is a need for this: formerly, once you'd officially adopted, you were on your own . . . just like any other parent. The national helpline from www.afteradoption.org.uk is 0800 0 568 578.

Later years

The later years can be just as challenging for you as the earlier trials. Although you now know your own strength – and you know how much you've helped your child, and can help again – you might still want some back-up, especially if contact is made with birth mother. There are other organisations that might be able to help, and they are listed at the end of the book.

Adults are independent

Remember that it's not the end of the world if your child wants to meet his or her birth mother. When they are 18, anything might happen – they might decide to move to the other end of the country or to the other side of the planet. There is no guarantee of proximity, nor of how they run their lives, or how often you'll see them . . . again, just like any other parent.

'Remember that it's not the end of the world if your child wants to meet his or her birth mother.'

Mental health first

My main concern for Clare as she grew to maturity was that despite all she'd been through she would emerge with psychological good health. I would expect that there would be mental health problems in the family background of any child who was a victim of abuse or neglect.

But there's no way of telling what will happen. For now, it's so far, so good.

Contact with siblings

Part of our adoption agreement was that Clare, one of five siblings, should maintain contact with the others as she grew up. They were all adopted by families in the West Country.

I enjoyed meeting the other adoptive parents – who all had children of their own. We arranged teas, days out, dinners at home and in restaurants. This was a marvellous link.

He's found!

Inevitably, this fell off as all the children reached 18 and beyond. Clare lost touch with her brother as he'd moved away from home – but found him again on Facebook when she was 30.

They then began to meet and renewed a bond. They spend every Christmas Day together and meet in-between.

'Facebook has both positive and negative effects. You might want to think twice about letting a young, newly-adopted child have a Facebook account. You'll be under a lot of pressure to let him or her have one, but I think it's asking for trouble well before you or your child will be ready to handle them.

Advice from our social worker, Sarah Acheson, on the teenage years: 'Don't make too many demands on the child. Things will change.'

Fitting in, and leaving home

It's possible that your child will begin to want to leave home, especially if there's been conflict. This certainly happened with Clare. Once she had her own flat, things changed so much . . . and for the better!

It was hard to believe a year or so later that the child who phoned us and asked us round for dinner was the same one who barely spoke to us for several years! My own feeling is that the child who has been in care longs desperately for their own space, perhaps more than children who have never been in that situation.

He or she has always been subject to other people's tastes. When they moved in with you, it's likely you created an 'ideal' space for them that they had to fit into, rather than a room they'd grown up with, with familiar toys and furniture.

'Facebook has both positive and negative effects. You might want to think twice about letting a young, newly-adopted child have a Facebook account.'

Need2Know

They were a transplant, their life joined quite suddenly with yours, and your tastes would dominate. So it's no wonder they love the idea of their own flat and furnishing it, being independent and being their own person.

Bright future

The future looks bright. We meet regularly. She asks us to dinner at her flat or meets me in town. Any problems, she is on the phone to us.

There's a sense that we've all been through an amazing experience with ups and downs, and we've grown and flourished. It's really worth doing – a privilege I'll never, ever, regret.

'There's a sense that we've all been through an amazing experience with ups and downs, and we've grown and flourished. It's really worth doing – a privilege I'll never, ever, regret.'

Summing Up

- At 18, your child is free to contact his or her birth mother.

- Sit with him or her while they read their social workers' early reports.

- Don't insist on seeing any letter they write to their birth mother.

- If they decide not to continue the links, remember they can always change their mind later.

- You can get post-adoption support when they're 18 and officially an adult – it's there for you.

- Encourage your child into independent living.

- Keep celebrating the adoption – it was an amazing thing for you all!

Adoption – FAQs

Can anyone adopt?

Adoption is open to anyone – married, single, same-sex couples. A criminal record does not bar you from adoption, but you are not permitted to adopt or foster children if you, your partner or any member of your household has been cautioned or convicted for any sexual or violent offence against a child. Any other offence against a child will also prohibit adoption.

Am I too old?

Adopters must be over 21 in England and Wales. But there's no upper age limit.

How long will it take to adopt?

The government is doing all it can to speed up the process, which it has described as 'overloaded with red tape' and 'painfully slow'. It also wants changes that will speed up and encourage more inter-racial adoptions. However, checks still need to be robust. The process varies from area to area, yet overall the speeding-up process is in place. The idea is for children to spend less time in care. In Harrow, London, all children are matched within six months, while in other regions potential adopters could still be waiting up to two years. This includes the assessment process, which can take eight months.

Could I continue working?

Yes, you can keep working, but ideally one parent should be able to give up work, at least temporarily, or work from home. As with any new parent, taking as much time to bond with your new child will pay dividends in the long run.

Can I still claim maternity/paternity allowance?

Yes. If your average weekly earnings are £87 or more (before tax), Statutory Adoption Pay is paid for a maximum of 39 weeks at £112.75 or 90 percent of your average weekly earnings if this is less.

Can I ask my employer if I can go from full-time to part-time hours when I adopt?

If you have worked for more than 26 weeks for the same employer you have a right to request flexible work arrangements. Your boss is legally obliged to consider the request seriously, but it can be turned down if there's a good business reason.

Must I be well off?

Adoption agencies need to see that you can support yourself and your family, but you don't need to be affluent.

Do I need to own my home?

No, you can be a home owner, council tenant or private tenant – all are acceptable.

I am a smoker/very overweight. Will this affect whether I can adopt?

There are no blanket bans on who can adopt in terms of physique or health. But your health and lifestyle is taken into account, as are the risks of passive smoking. This could affect your chances of adopting a baby, but not the opportunity to adopt an older child who would be at school during the day. Agencies will want to be sure you also need to have the energy and stamina to cope with children.

Do I need to have spent time looking after children?

You will be asked how much experience you've had in looking after children, or helping to. This could include time spent with young relatives or in your job if you deal with children in some way. It's always good to get some experience under your belt, and volunteering is a great tool for this. Try www.do-it.org.uk for lists of opportunities in volunteering in your area. You could volunteer in a playgroup, reading to children, mentoring and lots more.

What's the chance of adopting a baby?

Very slim – the average age a child placed for adoption in the UK is four years.

Can I improve my chances of adopting?

If you can take a sibling group – over half the children waiting to be adopted are in groups of brothers and sisters – or a child with a disability, you would definitely help your chances, provided all the other boxes are ticked.

Does it cost money to adopt?

Very little. You may need to pay for medicals and various certificates, and perhaps references, but this won't be much.

I have my own children already. Can I still adopt?

Yes, it makes no difference. But some children need to be adopted as an 'only child' because they need a lot of attention, and sometimes social workers will not place adopted children who are older than the existing children.

Are any adopted children voluntarily 'given up' by their birth parents?

Very few. The majority of children in the care system have been removed from birth parents for different reasons – usually for their own safety. These children are usually living with foster families.

Will our adopted child take our surname?

Once the adoption is complete – when a judge has signed the adoption order – the child becomes part of your family and normally would take your surname. But sometimes – as with the author of this book – the child will incorporate your surname into their own name, maybe as a middle name. An older child can be asked what they'd prefer to do.

I am not British – can I still adopt?

You can apply to adopt if your permanent home is in Britain or you've been a resident here for more than 12 months. You'll need to have solid proof of this.

Help List

Adoption UK

www.adoptionuk.org
Run by and for adopters, this website offers self-help informaton, advice,
support and tips to make adoption succeed. Support before, during and after
the adoption process.

Adoption UK Scotland

www.adoptionuk.org./info/Scotland
Masses of information and resources for prospective adopters living in

Scotland

BBC

www.bbc.co.uk/health/support/fostering/_adoption/ Are you eligible to adopt?
You can find out here, plus learn what adoption entails.

British Association for Adoption and Fostering

www.baaf.org.uk
British Association for Adoption and Fostering (BAAF) has a website which is
packed with information – the first port of call for would-be adopters.
www.bemyparent.org.uk
BAAF info pack, events, video clips and children's profiles.

Citizens Information

www.citizensinformation.ie/birth_family
Extensive information on adopting in Ireland.

Directgov

www.directgov/uk/eng/parents/moneyandwork
Information on adoption leave and adoption pay for workers.

Do-it

www.do-it.org.uk

Find charities close to you which can give you a taste of working with children.

International Adoption Guide

www.internationaladoptionguide.co.uk

All about inter-country adoption into the UK.

Thinking Of Adopting

www.thinkingofadopting.com

Geared for the US, but worth a look.

Booklist

Adopting a Child
By Jenifer Lord, BAAF, London 2001

Adopting Large Sibling Groups
By Hilary Saunders and Julie Selwyn, BAAF, London 2011

An Adoption Diary
By Maria James, BAAF, London 2006

Brothers and Sisters in Adoption
By Arleta James, Jessica Kingsley Publishers London 2012

Building the Bonds of Attachment
By Daniel A Hughes, published by Jason Aranson, USA 2006

Guiding You Through the Adoption Process
By Adoption UK, London £4 95
(This book is free if you join www.adoptionuk.org)

The Adopter's Handbook
By Amy Neil Salter, BAAF, London 2011

The Primal Wound: Understanding the Adopted Child
By Nancy Newton Verrier, Lafayette, Gateway Press USA 1993

Magazine: Adoption Now
At £4.95 per issue crammed with research and support for adoptive families
from www.adoptionuk.org

Need - 2 - Know

Available Titles Include ...

Allergies A Parent's Guide
ISBN 978-1-86144-064-8 £8.99

Autism A Parent's Guide
ISBN 978-1-86144-069-3 £8.99

Blood Pressure The Essential Guide
ISBN 978-1-86144-067-9 £8.99

Dyslexia and Other Learning Difficulties
A Parent's Guide ISBN 978-1-86144-042-6 £8.99

Bullying A Parent's Guide
ISBN 978-1-86144-044-0 £8.99

Epilepsy The Essential Guide
ISBN 978-1-86144-063-1 £8.99

Your First Pregnancy The Essential Guide
ISBN 978-1-86144-066-2 £8.99

Gap Years The Essential Guide
ISBN 978-1-86144-079-2 £8.99

Secondary School A Parent's Guide
ISBN 978-1-86144-093-8 £9.99

Primary School A Parent's Guide
ISBN 978-1-86144-088-4 £9.99

Applying to University The Essential Guide
ISBN 978-1-86144-052-5 £8.99

ADHD The Essential Guide
ISBN 978-1-86144-060-0 £8.99

Student Cookbook – Healthy Eating The Essential Guide
ISBN 978-1-86144-069-3 £8.99

Multiple Sclerosis The Essential Guide
ISBN 978-1-86144-086-0 £8.99

Coeliac Disease The Essential Guide
ISBN 978-1-86144-087-7 £9.99

Special Educational Needs A Parent's Guide
ISBN 978-1-86144-116-4 £9.99

The Pill An Essential Guide
ISBN 978-1-86144-058-7 £8.99

University A Survival Guide
ISBN 978-1-86144-072-3 £8.99

View the full range at **www.need2knowbooks.co.uk**.
To order our titles call **01733 898103**, email **sales@ n2kbooks.com** or visit the website. Selected ebooks available online.

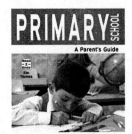

Need - 2 - Know, Remus House, Coltsfoot Drive, Peterborough, PE2 9BF